# STAGEC
# TRAVEL

## Louise Allen

SHIRE PUBLICATIONS

Published in Great Britain in 2014 by Shire Publications Ltd,
PO Box 883, Oxford, OX1 9PL, UK.
PO Box 3985, New York, NY 10185-3985, USA.

E-mail: shire@shirebooks.co.uk www.shirebooks.co.uk

A CIP catalogue record for this book is available from the
British Library.

Shire Library no. 789. ISBN-13: 978 0 74781 366 8
PDF ebook ISBN: 978 0 74781 537 2
e-pub ISBN: 978 0 74781 536 5

Louise Allen has asserted her right under the Copyright,
Designs and Patents Act, 1988, to be identified as the
author of this book.

Designed by Tony Truscott Designs, Sussex, UK and
typeset in Perpetua and Gill Sans.

Printed in China through Worldprint Ltd.

14 15 16 17 18    10 9 8 7 6 5 4 3 2 1

COVER IMAGE
Cover design and photography by Peter Ashley. Royal Mail
coach (pre-1840) in the Mossman Collection, courtesy
of the Stockwood Discovery Centre, Luton. Back cover
detail: *August*, from William Nicholson's *An Almanac of
Twelve Sports* 1898.

TITLE PAGE IMAGE
A stagecoach arrives at the Bell inn at Stilton,
Cambridgeshire, on the Great North Road. Stilton cheese,
although not made in the village, was served in the inns
and sold to passengers, spreading its fame across the
country.

CONTENTS PAGE IMAGE
The Brighton to London safety coach on the Marine
Parade, Brighton. There are no rooftop seats and the
outside passengers sit in a compartment behind the
enclosed carriage. With its lower centre of gravity,
this type of coach would be more stable than other
contemporary coaches.

ACKNOWLEDGEMENTS
Permission to reproduce illustrations are gratefully
acknowledged as follows:

Getty Images, page 10 (top); Mary Evans Picture Library,
pages 14–15, 26, 31, 34, 35, 47 (bottom), 50–1, 56, 60.

Permission to take photographs is gratefully acknowledged
as follows:

Birmingham Museums Service, pages 28 (bottom),
40 (bottom), 47 (top); Mossiman Collection, Luton
Museums Service, cover, page 29 (top); Red House
Stables Carriage Museum, pages 24 (bottom), 28 (top),
30 (bottom), 33, 34, 36 (top), 41 (bottom), 57 (top);
Swingletrees Carriage Driving Centre, page 10 (bottom).

All photographs are copyright A. J. Hilton. The remaining
images are from the author's collection.

Shire Publications is supporting the Woodland Trust, the UK's leading woodland conservation charity, by funding the dedication of trees.

# CONTENTS

# THE FIRST STAGECOACHES

THE FIRST STAGECOACHES appeared in the mid-seventeenth century. Expensive, unreliable, uncomfortable and beset with dangers, they crawled along the appalling roads, and prudent passengers made their wills before setting out. Yet by 1820 a golden age had dawned for stage- and mail-coach travel, one that was to last only until the 1840s, when the railways killed not just an industry but an entire way of life.

The stage and mail coaches were a driving force of the Industrial Revolution. They stimulated improvements to roads; they brought news to remote areas, accurate timekeeping to villages, employment to thousands, and affordable transport for many.

The name 'stagecoach' is descriptive: a coach is a four-wheeled passenger vehicle with more than one seat, and with the roof forming part of the framing of the body; a stage is the distance between predetermined stopping points for changing horses. Stage wagons, slow goods vehicles with very wide wheels to cope with the roads, were already transporting goods and passengers by the time the first known stagecoach, pulled by six heavy horses, set out to travel the 182 miles from London to Chester in 1657 for a fare of £1 15s for the six-day journey.

Communication at the time was easiest by water – by sea, rivers and, later, canals. Roads, sketchily maintained by individual parishes, were poor at best, lethal at worst. As late as 1770 Arthur Young wrote: '*To Wigan*. I know not in the whole range of language terms sufficiently expressive to describe this infernal road … [It has] ruts, which I actually measured four feet deep.'

But the country was changing. Industrial and technical developments were transforming manufacturing, trade and society, and triggering a relentless shift from a rural to an urban economy, with a resulting increase in population.

By the mid-eighteenth century communications were at a tipping point. Economic and industrial development required faster, reliable, connections

Opposite: An eighteenth-century stagecoach rolls away under the ornate sign for the White Hart inn, Scole, Norfolk. The sign, erected in 1655, had been taken down by the nineteenth century, but the inn is still there.

5

Sir Henry Parnell, in his *Treatise on Roads* (1838), writes that 'Milestones are convenient and agreeable to travellers, and useful in enabling coachmen to keep their time with accuracy'. This handsome example stands where the Old North Road joins the Great North Road at Alconbury, Cambridgeshire.

between towns and cities. Conflicts on the Continent, culminating in years of war with France, were a further stimulus, as was the trade generated by the growing empire. Gradually the realisation dawned on government that improving the roads themselves, rather than trying to regulate the vehicles using them, was the only way to secure speed and reliability.

Private turnpike trusts, improving roads in return for charging a toll at regular intervals, began piecemeal in the mid-eighteenth century. Finally, after about 1809, the new science of road-making, pioneered by Thomas Telford and perfected by John Macadam, allowed the turnpikes to spread across the entire country.

This book explores the experience of stagecoach travel in Britain from the point of view of the passengers, outlining their choice of routes and coaching company, their reasons for travelling, and the business of booking and joining the stagecoach, before moving on to the vital components of the experience – the coach itself, the coachman and guard, and the horses. Then, once the coach is under way, it describes the journey itself, the inns along the way and the dangers travellers faced.

An early stagecoach being driven 'unicorn' – that is drawn by three horses with a postilion on the leader. The rooftop passengers have a rail to hold on to, while others sit in the basket. Being 'in the basket' became slang for being penniless.

# THE GROWTH OF THE BUSINESS

THE NETWORK of stagecoach routes developed slowly between a few major cities, and at first they existed in isolation, with no onward service to connect the travellers with their ultimate destination, other than their own feet or hired horses and carriages. Only a handful of people with a pressing need to travel and a significant amount of money in their purses experienced these early vehicles.

In 1667 the first known stagecoach advertisement appeared:

Flying Machine
All those desirous to pass from London to Bath, or any other Place on their Road, let them repair to the Bell Savage on Ludgate Hill in London, and the White Lion in Bath, at both which places they may be received in a Stage Coach every Monday, Wednesday and Friday, which performs the Whole Journey in Three Days (if God permit) and sets forth at five o'clock in the morning. Passengers to pay One Pound five Shillings each ...

By 1675 we know of six English routes, and in 1678 Scotland's first stagecoach connected Edinburgh and Glasgow, a distance of 41 miles. Stages were long, and therefore journeys were slow, because the system of stabling relief horses at regular intervals had not yet been developed and overnight rests were therefore needed.

As roads slowly improved during the eighteenth century, and the staging of horses was better organised, more routes spread from London, first to Oxford and Cambridge, then to the Midlands and the West. Eventually the stagecoaches reached north to Carlisle and Edinburgh.

The development of lighter, better-designed vehicles from about 1730 helped both to increase speed and attract demand, and travel by stagecoach became a more viable proposition. Advertisements for 'flying machines' implied amazing speeds, even though the roads were too uneven, and the vehicles themselves too unreliable, to allow arrival times to be promised,

Overleaf:
A mid-eighteenth-century stage drives towards London in a cloud of dust.

An advertisement of 1717 for the Henley to London service.

The London to Norwich mail coach. The number, 205, signified the mail coach route and the cipher 'GR' below the coachman's box is for George IV. The crown on the door and the picture of the Order of the Garter star on the rear panel emphasise the fact that this is the Royal Mail.

and all of these journeys were advertised as 'barring accidents' or 'God permitting'. The Bath stage in the 1780s may have been the first to run to a schedule, a sign of growing professionalism by stagecoach proprietors.

With these improvements, reliability became the expectation, not the exception. In 1763 there was one coach between Edinburgh and London. It left once a month and took between twelve and fourteen days. By the 1830s there were six or seven coaches each way daily, and a journey time of under forty-eight hours.

Another influence on speed and reliable scheduling was the mail coach service started by

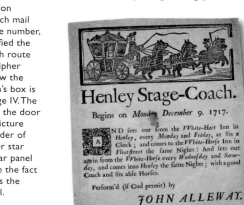

## Henley Stage-Coach.

Begins on Monday December 9. 1717.

AND sets out from the VVhite-Hart Inn in Henley, every Monday and Friday, at Six a Clock; and comes to the VVhite-Horse Inn in Fleetstreet the same Nights: And sets out again from the VVhite-Horse every Wednesday and Saturday, and comes into Henley the same Nights; with a good Coach and Six able Horses.

Perform'd (if God permit) by

### JOHN ALLEWAY.

NOTE, The Stage will begin to go three times a Week, from the 25th of March next ensuing, during the Summer-Season. Likewise, That they do call at the Black-Bear in Piccadilly every Journey.

John Palmer, MP for Bath, in 1784. He owned playhouses in Bath and Bristol, and his business suffered from the unreliable mail services — the post boy's ambling nag could take more than two days between Bristol and London. By using his own carriages Palmer demonstrated that the journey could be done in fourteen hours, at just over 8 mph, and he convinced the government to approve official mail coaches running 10-mile stages. Although essentially similar to stagecoaches, and run by private contractors, the mail coaches had the monopoly of carrying mail and official documents and were governed by the Post Office regulations concerning timetables, security and staff behaviour. From the beginning their design was standardised.

Stagecoach travel became a viable option for anyone except the poor. Increased speed and greater safety and reliability were achieved through improved roads, lighter, better-designed coaches, improved harnesses, shorter stops, and shortening the distances between changes of horses from 20 miles in 1800 to 10 miles by the 1820s. Stagecoaches were taxed and licensed, which is useful for recording the growth of the industry. In 1814 there were 1,331 licensed stagecoaches; by 1835 there were 3,056.

In 1820, 145 years after six stagecoach routes were all a traveller could choose from, it has been calculated that there were 1,500 opportunities to leave London by stage or mail coach every twenty-four hours.

Once the network of main routes, the 'long-stages', was established, 'short-stages' developed to link up towns and to provide transport into the main hubs. These were often run by small proprietors such as innkeepers or farmers.

Around London short-stages developed rapidly from about 1815. By 1825 about six hundred London short-stages were making around 1,800 journeys daily, stopping when they reached 'the stones', the cobbled road surface which marked the territory of the hackney carriages, where passengers would change to hackneys or walk.

After the peace in 1815 there was even an international route from London to Paris. A direct coach, with a French-speaking courier, left from the George and Blue Boar in Holborn to Dover, where it was put on board a ship to Calais, before travelling on to Paris.

Stagecoaches were built by specialists, the contractors, who rented them to the

An advertisement of 1802 for the 'Cambridge & Birmingham University Coach', running cross-country between the two cities to link up with other major routes. Luggage is charged at one penny a pound and anything above £5 in value must be registered in advance.

SARACEN's-HEAD INN,
BULL-STREET, BIRMINGHAM.

SETS out from the above Inn, the ORIGINAL CAMBRIDGE & BIRMINGHAM UNIVERSITY COACH, every Tuesday Morning at Seven o'Clock, by Way of Coventry, Dunchurch, Daventry, to the Role-and-Crown Inn, Northampton, sleeps there; proceeds the next Morning through Wellingborough, Thrapston, and Huntingdon, to the Blue-Boar Inn, Cambridge, where it meets the Newmarket, Bury, and Ipswich Coaches.—Returns from the above Inn in Cambridge, every Thursday Morning at Six; will arrive in Birmingham on Friday Afternoon, in Time for the Bath, Bristol, and other Coaches.
   Performed by the Public's humble Servants,
                  WM. GIDDING, Birmingham.
         JER. BRIGGS, Northampton.
   Fares as usual.—Luggage to Cambridge, 1d. per Pound.
   *₊* The Proprietors of the above Coach return their most grateful Acknowledgments for Favours already received from a generous Public, and hope for the Continuance of that Patronage it will ever be their Study to merit, but cannot be accountable for any Article above 5l. Value (if lost) unless entered as such, and paid for accordingly.

This detail from John Cary's *Reduction of His Large Map of England and Wales* (1805) shows the coach routes around London. Roads served by both mail and stage services are shown in blue, those with only stagecoaches in red.

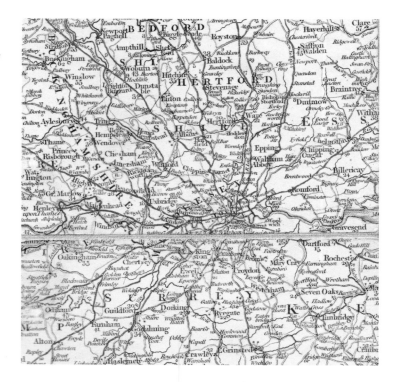

A water man, one of the essential workers necessary to maintain the thousands of horses used on the stage and mail routes.

proprietors, the men and women who managed the routes, provided the horses and the workforce, and owned or rented the inns that were the termini for the routes. The coaches would be returned to the contractors for repairs and regular maintenance.

The proprietors had to be skilled and ruthless entrepreneurs to win business as the number of routes grew and travellers had more options. Their coaches were moving advertisements, painted in their own livery colours and the names of the towns and inns at each end of the route. If a rival coach encroached on their run, they put on extra coaches to 'nurse' the route, running them immediately before and after the rival, and if competition became acrimonious they might encourage their drivers to race.

The stage and mail coaches supported a vast range of ancillary industries. There were the coachbuilders and their specialist staff; harness, whip and horn makers; tailors who made the uniforms for the staff; stable staff; horse dealers;

farmers providing feed and straw; farriers and blacksmiths and the inns and their whole network of servants and suppliers.

By the 1820s there were more than thirty thousand people directly or indirectly employed, and over 150,000 horses in use. With so many outgoings, the costs of running a long-stage coach route were enormous. The accounts for 1829 of a Lancashire company with thirty-three coaches show expenditure of £42,100 for rent and for the horses and their upkeep alone, before wages, tolls and taxes. The smaller proprietors were soon unable to afford the cut-throat long-stage business and specialised in the cross-country short-stages, leaving a few main proprietors in each large town.

LIST of INNS from which STAGE COACHES Depart.

*Belle Sauvage, Ludgate Hill.*

*Passengers and Parcels are forwarded from this Inn the same as from the* WHITE HORSE, *Fetter Lane, and* CROSS KEYS, *Wood Street.*

52. ALTON and FARNHAM, by Bagshot *(Itin.* 51, 52, to Bagshot; 71, to Alton). Tue. Thu. Sat. 9 morn. Ar. Swan, Alton, 5 aft. Dep. Mon. Wed. Fri. 9 morn. Ar. 4 aft.
53. BATH and BRISTOL, through Marlborough, Calne, and Chippenham *(Itin.* 131 to 136, to Bath; 159, to Bristol). Dai. 2 aft.
54. BRIGHTON. Dai ¾ p. 9 morn.
55. EPSOM and EWELL. Dai. 5 aft.
56. GOSPORT, thro' Fareham *(Itin.* 51, 52, to Bagshot; 71, to Alton; 85, to Gosport). Dai. 6 even.
57. MITCHAM and TOOTING. Dai. ¼ bef. 5, Sun. excepted.
58. NEWBURY and READING, through Maidenhead *(Itin.* 131 to 135). Dai. 6 morn. Sun. excepted. Ar. Wh. Hart, Newbury, 4 aft. Dep. 8 morn. Ar. 6 even.
59. PORTSMOUTH. Dai. 5 morn. and 5 even.
60. SALISBURY and ANDOVER, thro' Basingstoke *(Itin,* 51 to 55). Dai. ¼ p. 3 aft. Ar. Black Horse, Salisbury, 9 morn. Dep. 4 aft. Ar. 9 morn.
61. SOUTHAMPTON and WINCHESTER, thro' Bagshot, Farnham, Alton, and Alresford *(Itin.* 51, 52, to Bagshot; 71, 72, to Southampton). Dai. Sunday excepted, 4 morn. Ar. Star, Southampton, 6 even. Dep. 5 morn. Ar. ½ p. 6 even.
62. STOWE, CHIPPING NORTON, ENSTONE, and WOODSTOCK. Tu. Th. Sat. ½ p. 7 morn.
63. WELLS, SHEPTON MALLET, FROME, and WARMINSTER, by Salisbury. Tu. Th. Sun. 3 aft.
64. WINDSOR and ETON, 7 morn. and 1 aft.
65. WITNEY, thro' Oxford, Wheatley, Tetsworth, and Wycombe. Tu. Th. Sat. ¾ p. 7 morn.

In London there were six major proprietors. William Chaplin owned the Swan with Two Necks in Lad Lane, a famous and spectacular yard that attracted crowds of sightseers to watch the coaches depart. Chaplin maintained 1,800 horses and a staff of over two thousand to run his sixty-eight routes.

His great rival, Edward Sherman, was canny enough to marry three rich widows in succession and with their resources he bought the Bull and Mouth in St Martin's le Grand. His livery was bright yellow for maximum visibility and he had a booking office in Regent's Circus, the 'Western Coach Office'. In 1825 his *Shrewsbury Wonder* ran the route in fifteen hours and he stabled 150 horses for that coach alone. He prospered so well that in 1830 he rebuilt the Bull and Mouth, with extensive accommodation for passengers and underground stabling for seven hundred horses.

The Nelson family was led by the widowed Mrs Nelson from the Bull inn, Aldgate. Her coaches, which included the profitable Norwich coach, were always well-horsed, and she had a virtual monopoly of the routes to the eastern counties, as well as running the *Exeter Defiance*. By the 1830s she also owned the Spread Eagle in Gracechurch Street and had acquired Chaplin's Swan with Two Necks.

Her son Robert ran the Belle Sauvage on Ludgate Hill and controlled routes as widely spread as the *Star* coach to Cambridge and the *Red Rover* to Manchester, the coaches painted red with matching harness and red uniforms for the staff.

Another coaching widow was Mrs Mountain, running thirty coaches daily from the Saracen's Head. She inherited the business from her husband and, unusually, was also a contractor with her own coach factory.

Part of John Cary's *New Itinerary ... of the Great Roads* (1812 edition), listing the stagecoaches from the Belle Sauvage inn on Ludgate Hill in the City of London.

Overleaf: Edward Sherman's Western Coach Office in Regent's Circus. Passengers could book here for the thirty-three coaches he ran from the Bull and Mouth inn in the City.

# PASSENGERS, BOOKING AND DEPARTURE

By the early nineteenth century, with so much improvement in the infrastructure and fierce rivalry between companies, there was a choice of routes and coaches for anyone wanting to travel between most English towns, and between the major centres in Scotland, Wales and Ireland.

It was not cheap. Colonel Hawker and his servant took the London–Glasgow mail in 1812 and he recorded the fares and tips as totalling £19 10s, in addition to refreshments. However it was considerably less expensive than hiring a chaise or owning a carriage, and a wide range of passengers could afford it, if only occasionally.

Many travelled out of economic necessity, to seek work or to take up an appointment, and the improving stagecoach network enabled the shift of population from country to town. In 1767 Arthur Young wrote:

> Young men and women … enter into service in the country for little else but to raise money enough to go to London, which was no such easy matter when a stage-coach was four or five days in creeping a hundred miles. The fare and expenses ran high. *But now!* A country fellow, one hundred miles from London jumps on a coach box in the morning and for eight or ten shillings gets to town by night.

Servants and governesses taking up appointments would travel by coach, merchants and tradesmen found them convenient, and professional men such as lawyers, journalists and actors used them. The Shakespearean actor Charles Macready always travelled by stage and in 1834 he covered hundreds of miles on one extensive tour, including London, Cardiff, Bristol, Chepstow, Gloucester, Birmingham and Ireland.

As a young man Charles Dickens worked as a reporter on the *Morning Chronicle* and used stage and mail coaches extensively. He grumbled at the time about the discomforts, but looked back with nostalgia in his later writings.

Opposite:
A small crowd gathers to watch a mail coach getting ready to leave the General Post Office in London. The driver takes his seat while waiting for the last mail sack to be carried out, and a man offers oranges to the passengers on the roof.

This sketch of about 1816 shows respectably dressed passengers on the seat behind the coachman, and a lady with an umbrella who will be sitting next to him.

Children, especially schoolboys, would be sent off alone by stage. When eleven-year-old William Wordsworth travelled from Charterhouse School to his home in the Lake District, his mother wrote:

We have no fear of trusting him by the Mail — provided [her cousin or the headmaster] give him in charge either to the guard, the coachman or any respectable Passenger. People travelling are always kind to Children … only pray impress upon him that he is not to get upon the outside, and above all to avoid leaning over the doors of the Coach.

The expenses of Mr Oldman, a clerk on a business journey to London from Cumbria, using a wide variety of hired vehicles. He shared a chaise from Penrith to York, which came to £2 4s 8d, stayed overnight for 10s 6d, then caught the stagecoach at a cost of £3 3s, with 11s 6d for food and drink, 4s 6d for tips and 5s 6d for his luggage. In London he paid 6s for a room at the White Horse, Fetter Lane, with an additional 4s 11d in tips, for shaving water and for a hackney carriage to catch the Chertsey short-stage. His return trip on that cost 10s, and he finally caught the mail coach home to Penrith for £5, plus £1 for his luggage and £1 7s 9d for the various expenses of the journeys. Oldman claimed £13 9s 4d for travel and accommodation at a time when an agricultural labourer might earn about £12 a year.

Some passengers had no choice. Convicts were regularly transported by coach, and perhaps Dickens witnessed this, for Pip observes in *Great Expectations* that he had 'more than once seen them on the high roads dangling their ironed legs over the coach roof.' In 1818 Mary Wordsworth wrote in some distress that she had boarded the stage at Manchester before it stopped at the House of Correction, where ten convicts in shackles bound for Lancaster Gaol and transportation abroad were loaded on to the roof. The coach was surrounded by weeping wives and children. 'It saddened the day,' she commented.

The Greyhound, Cromford, Derbyshire, built in the eighteenth century by Sir Richard Arkwright to provide accommodation for the businessmen and foreign visitors who flocked to his pioneering spinning factories. Stagecoaches left from the market square in front.

As coach travel became more reliable, and the Romantic Movement engendered an interest in picturesque and dramatic scenery, a tourist industry developed. *The Guide to the Watering and Sea-Bathing Places* for 1818 gives details of stagecoach connections for each resort so that tourists could plan their stay. For Eastbourne, for example, it notes, 'There are two good inns, the Lamb and the New Inn, where proper attention is paid to guests … A stage coach goes to and from London thrice a week during the summer months, and a post daily.'

In 1795 a Scottish minister, the Reverend William MacRitchie, kept a diary as he toured England by stagecoach, sitting outside for the best view

A stagecoach arrives in Brighton and turns into Marine Parade amidst crowds of sightseers.

The *Birmingham Wonder* passes a country house. The American Benjamin Silliman observed in 1805: 'At intervals of a mile or two, beautiful country seats adorned the road [to Bath], and with their forests, their parks, their sloping fields, and their herds of deer, presented a most interesting succession of objects.'

when the weather permitted. On seeing the City of London from Highgate Hill, he exclaimed, 'Heav'ns! What a goodly prospect spreads around!' He was also an amateur botanist and when he observed interesting plants on the road to Cambridge he lamented he could not stop and look at them. Another tourist, James Losh, went by stage into the Lake District in 1816. 'The drive up the Lake of Windermere ... filled my mind with a pleasing tranquillity', he wrote.

Fashionable passengers might be seen on certain routes, especially the Brighton road. The Brighton coaches became notorious for flirtations, and on fine summer days pretty girls and young bucks would sit outside on facing seats, enjoying a party all the way from London to the coast.

Some of those rooftop flirtations may have led to love affairs. Certainly the stage and mail coaches were popular with eloping couples making haste to the border and a Scottish marriage. An average of two couples a day arrived at Gretna Green, usually on the 6 a.m. coach, but any route that led into Scotland would do. When Percy Bysshe Shelley eloped with Harriet Westbrook in August 1811 they took the Edinburgh mail. It was an unromantic experience, for she was travel-sick and he was broke, having forgotten to budget for the cost of the extras involved in coach travel.

The short-stage coaches around London served the first commuters. The American Louis Simond, travelling in 1810, observed: 'People live in the outskirts of the town in better air, larger houses, and at a smaller rent, and stages passing every half hour facilitate communications.' One commuter was the actor Charles Macready, who travelled on Billing's two-horse stage between Elstree, where he lived, and the London theatres where he performed.

### BOOKING A SEAT

Whatever their reason for travelling, the prospective passengers had to decide on a route and choose a coaching company. There were volumes of

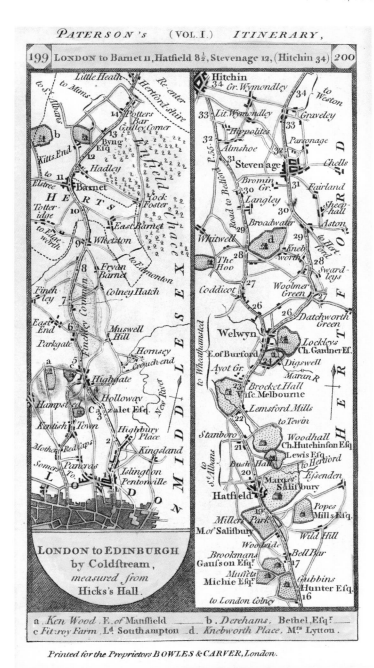

This strip map from *Paterson's Itinerary* (1793) shows the beginning of the Great North Road from London to Edinburgh. Road books of this sort were useful for travellers planning their journey.

An agitated passenger and an indifferent booking-office clerk.

advice to warn of the various pitfalls, and maps and road books to help with planning, such as Cary's *New Itinerary ... of the Great Roads*, Paterson's *Roads* and Gray's *The Tourist and Traveller's Guide to the Roads*, all of which went into numerous editions.

At 4d to 5d a mile inside, 2d a mile outside, prices varied little between companies, so the choice depended on timings, reputation and advertising. The unwary had to take care that booking clerks did not send them on an expensive, roundabout route. Thomas Carlyle warned in 1830: 'There are men in Liverpool who will *book* you to go by any Coach you like, and to enter London at any place and any hour you like; and *send* you thither by any Coach or combination of Coaches *they* like.'

Booking could be done at the inn from which the coach departed or from a booking office, such as the Western Coach Office in Regent's Circus.

'The Consequences of Being Too Late'. This gentleman with his trunk, portmanteau and picnic basket waves his umbrella in vain.

Passengers wait to be picked up by the stagecoach on a snowy Christmas Eve.

Or a passenger could arrange to be picked up at a specific place, through an agent at an inn along the route. Normally half the fare had to be paid in advance, with no refunds if the coach was missed.

In 1810 Louis Simond described a journey between Richmond and London:

> This morning I set out by myself for *town* … in the stagecoach, crammed inside, and *herissé* [like a hedgehog] outside with passengers, of all sexes, ages, and conditions. We stopped more than twenty times on the road – the debates about the fare of way-passengers – the settling themselves – the getting up, and the getting down, and damsels shewing their petticoats – complaining and swearing – took an immense time. I never saw anything so ill-managed. In about two hours we reached Hyde Park Corner.

It was sometimes possible to travel illicitly for a short distance, at a reduced fare split between driver and guard, which may be what Simond observed. This was called 'shouldering' and proprietors turned a blind eye to it. At the annual May Day dinner for his coachmen, William Chaplin's toast was 'Here's to shouldering – but don't let me catch you at it!'

In *Sketches by Boz*, Dickens recalled booking as an unpleasant experience:

> You enter a mouldy-looking room, ornamented by large posting-bills, the greater part of the place enclosed behind a huge lumbering rough counter,

The passengers gather in the inn yard and a vendor wearing a white apron carries a basket of wares on his head.

and fitted up with recesses ... Some half-dozen people are 'booking' brown-paper parcels, which one of the clerks flings into the aforesaid recesses with an air of recklessness ... porters, looking like so many Atlases, keep rushing in and out with large packages on their shoulders ... [one of the clerks] with his hat half off his head, enters the passengers' names in his books with a coolness which is inexpressibly provoking; and the villain whistles – actually whistles – while a man asks him what the fare is outside all the way to Holyhead!

### THE COACH DEPARTS

The coach would wait for no one but departed exactly according to schedule. The mails in particular were so punctual that villagers set their clocks by them. William Kitchener, in *The Traveller's Oracle or, Maxims for Locomotion*, advised:

> Secure a Place a Day or two before you set off ... It is necessary to be at the place in due Time; for, as the saying is, 'Time and Tide', and it may be added, 'Stage Coaches, stay for no Man'. As clocks vary, you will do wisely to *be there full five minutes before what you believe to be the true Time.*

A busy coaching terminus must have seemed chaotic, although the staff knew exactly what was needed to get the coach out on time and pushed their way efficiently through sightseers, hawkers, confused passengers and porters.

The scene at the White Horse Cellar or at the Gloucester Coffeehouse in Piccadilly before the West Country mails set off was recalled by Lord William Pitt Lennox:

> What a Babel of tongues! People hurrying hither and thither, some who had come too soon, others too late. There were carriages, hackney coaches, vans, carts and barrows; porters jostling, touters swearing, cads elbowing, coachmen wrangling, passengers grumbling, men pushing, women scolding.

A crutch used to shove passengers up on to the roof of the coach, an undignified procedure.

Trunks, portmanteaux, hat-boxes, band-boxes, strewed the pavement; orange merchants, cigar merchants, umbrella merchants ... perambulating piemen, coachmen out of a place, country clods, town cads – gaping, talking, wondering; the din occasionally interrupted by a street serenade, the trampling of cattle, or the music of the guard's horn.

The horn would sound as the coach left, but Mrs Nelson also employed guards who were experts in the key-bugle and set them to play a selection of tunes in the yard of the Bull to entertain travellers.

When the passengers had arrived on time, located their coach and tipped their porter and the guard, there was still the business of getting themselves and their luggage on board and finding the best possible seat. Kitchener recommended:

> On your arrival at the Coach Office, give your trunks, etc, in charge to the Coachman, and see them placed safely where they may not be rubbed ... Persons have their choice of Places in the order they get into the coach first, a Place so taken remaining with the Possessor the whole of the Journey.
>
> People are generally anxious to secure *Front places,* either because they cannot, or fancy they cannot ride backwards; but if they travel at Night, the Wind and Rain, while sitting in front, will beat into their faces, the only remedy for which is to draw up the Glasses (a privilege vested by travelling etiquette in the occupiers of those places) and thus must they sit the remainder of the Night in an Atmosphere too impure for any gentleman ...

A gentleman watches anxiously as his baggage is stowed in the boot.

Finally everyone was on board, the luggage stowed, the coachman ready to depart, and the watching crowd could enjoy the spectacle. William Cobbett wrote:

> Next to a fox hunt the finest sight in England is a stage coach just ready to start ... The vehicle itself, the harness, all so complete and so neatly arranged, so strong and clean and good; the beautiful horses, impatient to be off; the inside full and the outside covered, in every part, with men, women and children, boxes, bags, bundles ...

# THE COACH, ITS CREW AND HORSES

THE FIRST STAGECOACHES were lumbering unsprung vehicles with hard seats for six inside passengers. There were no seats for the outside passengers, who had to cling to the rounded top of the vehicle; they had no hand-hold until the 1750s, when rails were added. There were still no seats outside until, as the *London Evening Post* reported in 1751, the 'conveniency' or 'rumble-tumble', a vast wicker basket, was added for luggage and outside passengers. Passengers sat in it on straw and luggage but those on the roof were still in constant danger of falling off. C. P. Moritz, in *Travels through Various Parts of England* (1782), wrote: 'By what means passengers thus fasten themselves securely on the roof of these vehicles, I know not; but you constantly see numbers seated there, apparently at their ease.'

Improvements in design were stimulated by competition. By the 1750s 'glass coaches', fitted with glazed windows, were operating on the London to Edinburgh routes and from then on improvement was continual. It was found that smaller front wheels and better axles made the vehicle more manoeuvrable and stable, easier to drive and more comfortable to travel in. However, this was all aimed at increasing the speed, reliability and money-making potential of the vehicle by making it stronger, lighter and better able to carry passengers and luggage. Comfort was very much a secondary consideration.

By the early nineteenth century a coach cost over £100 to build. The basic structure was robust and the exterior finish was superb. Many coats of paint and varnish were applied, and the vehicles were decorated with their name, the route and their ownership. The names of coaches were designed to impress, implying speed or reliable time-keeping, such as *Lightning*, *Greyhound*, *Arrow*, *Constant* and *Chronometer*. Also popular, especially on the Brighton run, were royal names, including *Regent*, *Crown Prince* and *Royal Sovereign*, and Scottish coaches exploited the popularity of Sir Walter Scott's novels with names such as *Rob Roy* and *Antiquary*.

The body of these more elaborate coaches was about 13 feet long. The coachman's seat had some padding – but not much, in case he got too

Opposite:
A 'swell dragman',
one of the smart
new breed of
coachmen of the
1820s and '30s.

Right: The *Gay Gordon* stagecoach used on the London to Edinburgh run from 1832. In keeping with the popular Scottish theme, the panels are painted in a tartan pattern. This coach, a late model, has lever brakes that act directly on the rear wheels, but the chain of a drag shoe can also be seen. Between the two sets of roof seats there are straps for the central stack of baggage.

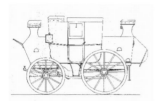

Above: An ideal stagecoach, shown in Sir Henry Parnell's *A Treatise on Roads* (1838).

comfortable and fell asleep – and there was room for one passenger beside him. Behind them there was a seat facing forwards, with another at the back facing the guard. The luggage would be piled up between these two seats.

The mail coaches weighed 1 ton empty, half a ton lighter than the stagecoaches. By law they maintained a speed of 10 mph and they were famously reliable, so that the up mail and the

The Chester to London *Old Times* stagecoach in the Birmingham Museums Service store.

down mail on any route would always pass at the same point. They carried fewer outside passengers (none facing the guard for security reasons) and only four inside. At first they all sported the same livery of blue and orange, later changed to black and maroon, with the royal coat of arms and the names of their termini on the side. All of them were built by Vidler of London until 1835.

Accidents and competition were two of the factors in improving stagecoach design. John Vidler's *Telegraph* incorporated a number of innovations, including improved springing, afterwards known as 'Telegraph springs'. Faced with stiff competition from Edward Sherman on one route, Robert Nelson introduced the *Beehive* coach. He boasted: 'The inside of the coach is fitted up with spring cushions and a reading-lamp, lighted with wax, for the accommodation of those who wish to amuse themselves on the road.' It had numbered seat tickets and no fish was carried – presumably an unpleasantly smelly cargo on other coaches. Despite this, Sherman eventually won the business on the route.

A variety of 'safety coaches' were tried, such as the low-slung *Sovereign* on the Brighton road. Most of these had no rooftop seating, smaller wheels and a longer body.

But, despite all this, 'The convenience of travellers has been very little attended to in arranging the size of the bodies, and the height and depth of the seats inside coaches,' concluded Sir John Robisson, Secretary to the Edinburgh Royal Society. He recommended that seats should have

The door of the York to London mail coach in the Mossiman Collection, showing the royal coat of arms and the maroon livery.

The driver of the Sevenoaks to Tunbridge Wells coach is 'springing 'em' to take the hill while a passenger throws coins to small boys.

The memorial in Haddiscoe church, Norfolk, to William Salter, killed when his coach overturned on the hill below the church.

4-inch-thick cushions and be 18 inches deep to provide support to the thighs, and that seat backs should slope to support the spine. Little notice was taken of his advice.

## THE COACHMAN

The safety of the coach and its passengers and its punctual arrival depended on the coachman, a character who acquired prestigious status in a society where good horsemanship was of as much popular interest as football is today.

Coachmen, especially those on the long-stage routes, were admired by everyone from small boys to sporting gentlemen. In the early days they were hard-drinking, coarse, tough, swaggering and dictatorial men with weathered complexions and superb skills with horses. Washington Irving, an admirer of the profession, described one: '[It was] as if the blood had been forced with hard feeding into every vessel of his skin.'

Their characteristic clothing, designed to protect them on their exposed perch, was epitomised by the outermost of the many coats they wore. This reached to the heels, had multiple shoulder capes and was known from 1817 as a benjamin, after the tailor who made them. They set this off with huge mother-of-pearl buttons and also wore a broad-brimmed, low-crowned hat, a coloured neckerchief, a vividly striped waistcoat and low 'jockey' boots – a style of dress copied by the rich, sporting 'Corinthians'.

A coachman had to be tough. On long-stage routes they would drive for seven or eight hours at a time, covering 60 to 100 miles before handing over to the next man. This life was not conducive to domesticity, and most coachmen were unmarried, with a swashbuckling reputation amongst the female staff at inns.

The driver's seat of the Gay Gordon stagecoach showing a lap rug and the fixing for his whip. The coachman would keep the replaceable tips for his whip – the 'whip points' – between his teeth, which were often filed down to make this easier.

The coachman drove on the left and sat on the right, giving him the best line of sight down the crown of the road, and room to use his long whip on his team of four – or anyone getting in his way. He kept his horses at the trot for the most part, which was easiest on the horses, safest, and yielded speeds of 8–10 mph. Galloping increased the speed only to 13 mph and exhausted the horses, so it could not be sustained for any great distance and was reserved for the few excellent stretches of road, such as Hounslow to Staines, for taking a hill or, dangerously, for racing.

Despite his skills and responsibility, a coachman was not well paid. The sum of 18–20s a week was comparable to an agricultural labourer's wages, and out of that he was expected to pay the horse-keepers 1s a week. He would also be fined for any damage to the vehicle, loss of time or misdemeanours. However, an enterprising coachman expected to make considerably more from tips and various schemes.

Extracting tips was called 'shelling' or 'kicking' and involved approaching each passenger with outstretched hand and the words 'I'm leaving you now, sir'.

'The Oxford Coachman' of 1808. He is carrying his benjamin, a many-caped overcoat.

A coachman expected 2s 6d for every 50 miles, and the average annual income from tips was estimated as £300. Sporting gentlemen who wanted to 'take the ribbons' and 'wagon it', that is, drive the coach, would be expected to tip very handsomely for the privilege, enough, no doubt, to cover the fine of between £5 and £10 if it was reported by one of the numerous informers along the way.

Some coachmen provided horses for a few stages, and there was the income from taking up passengers who were not on the waybill ('shouldering'). They also often acted as tipsters and bookmakers.

By the early nineteenth century, with better roads and lighter, faster coaches, a number of gentlemen became professional drivers, either because they were out of pocket and driving was their only marketable skill, or for the sheer love of it. Henry Stevenson, a Cambridge graduate, drove his own coaches, *The Water Witch* from 1823 and then *The Age*, on the Brighton road. It was an elegant vehicle and its teams always consisted of a roan, a chestnut, a skewbald and a dun wearing silver-plated harness. Stops were enlivened with elegant refreshments offered by servants in livery. When Stevenson died, aged thirty, *The Age* was bought by Sir St Vincent Cotton, impoverished by gambling, who estimated he made £500 a year from it. Other well-born coachmen included the Marquis of Worcester and the Reverend Dennis, who left his Berkshire parish to drive the *White Hart* on the Bath road.

From the 1820s there was a change in the calibre of coachmen, with the rise of the 'swell dragmen' – smart, highly skilled and sober. The proprietors recruited more respectable men, including the sons of yeomen and merchants, and ex-military men, or trained young drivers up from scratch.

The son of John Buzzard, the coachman of the *Oxonian*, recalled this new breed of coachmen as 'intelligent, pleasant and, as a general rule, civil, obliging, and always well dressed'. His father 'would make his jokes as he drove along, or say something quaint to the horses, and at all times endeavour to keep his passengers in a merry mood'. Some could not resist jokes at the expense of passengers, such as asking them to bet which of the Six Hills ancient burial mounds on the Great North Road through Stevenage were furthest apart. The more gullible failed to realise it was the first and the last until it was too late.

A stagecoach passes through a tollgate.

They were certainly not all paragons. Sam Hayward, driver of the *Shrewsbury Wonder*, was notorious for taking the steep hill of Wyle Cop at the gallop, turning the horses sharply and driving through the archway into the yard of the Lion, with the terrified passengers on the roof having to lie flat to avoid being swept off.

## THE GUARD

Unlike the coachman, the guard remained with the coach for the whole journey, which might mean twenty-four hours on duty. He had to be reliable, fit and good with people, for his duties included taking tickets, organising the passengers, stowing the luggage, and keeping timesheets and records. He had to be honest, as he paid the tollgate keepers, and he required steady nerves to handle his blunderbuss. He had a toolkit and spare parts for running repairs, and an axe for clearing blockages on the road, and it was his job to apply the chain or skidpan to the rear wheels to brake the coach on hills.

In December 1815 the *Star* newspaper reported a 'Dreadful Accident' where the horses had bolted and overturned the coach. The coachman and a passenger died and several more passengers were badly injured. 'The guard, perceiving his perilous situation, let himself down from the back of the coach, and was so slightly injured, that he had self-possession enough to cut the traces which, in all probability, prevented even more serious injury to the passengers.'

A selection of chains and shoes used to slow coaches on hills. It was the guard's job to put these in place and remove them with the minimum of delay, a skilled and dangerous job that was usually done with the coach in motion.

The Holyhead to London mail, built c. 1826. The figure is wearing an original guard's uniform jacket and next to it is the wickerwork holder for the horn.

The guard blew a horn to warn the tollgates and inns of the approach of the coach or to alert vehicles they were about to be overtaken, and some guards also carried a curved horn with three keys to play popular tunes to entertain the passengers. For all this, he might expect to earn between 10s 6d and 15s weekly, plus his uniform, although his tips could bring him about £200 a year and he expected 2s 6d from each passenger for every hundred miles.

A mail-coach guard had the same duties and also had to be prepared to defend the mails with his life, armed with his blunderbuss and a cutlass. If the coach could not proceed, his orders were to take the mail sack and continue himself, whatever the weather. He was 'answerable at his peril for the security, safe conduct, and delivery of [the letter-bags] sealed', according to the official rules, all for a salary of 10s per week, rising to 30s after long service, plus tips. His uniform of red coat, blue waistcoat and cocked hat with gold braid was also provided.

A guard had other ways of supplementing his income and would act as a message service for notes and small packages, holding out his hat for them to be dropped in as the coach passed. John Walker, proprietor of *The Times* newspaper, lived in Bracknell and used the coaches as an unofficial mail service to send drafts and instructions to the London office.

In this 1832 print the guard loads a Birmingham stagecoach with an assortment of luggage while the horses are led out for the start of the run. He wears a pouch for money and waybills across his chest.

Carrying the news, and even newspapers, was a sure way to earn tips. When a stagecoach, covered in laurel wreaths, brought the news of the British victory at Waterloo to Glasgow, it galloped along Gallowgate to the main post office with the guard sounding his bugle, and when they reached Nelson Street he discharged his blunderbuss into the air. The guard of the London–Hereford *Mazeppa* recalled that in 1832, as the Reform Bill went through Parliament, he sold copies of *The Times* for up to 2 guineas in villages along the route.

Some guards were even more enterprising. An Exeter to London mail-coach guard admitted carrying a live calf in the boot because the price of veal in London was so high, and on another occasion a mail-coach superintendent declared that 'such a thing as a turtle tied to the roof directed to any gentleman once or twice a year might pass unnoticed, but for a constancy cannot be suffered'. The turtle would have been alive.

A 3-foot-long coach horn – the 'yard of tin'.

### THE HORSES

By the mid-eighteenth century passengers would expect to see four horses harnessed to their coach, although an extra pair with a postilion on a lead horse was used in very heavy going or thick snow.

The exciting spectacle of a stagecoach during a change of horses – a highly skilled operation taking only fifty seconds to two minutes – disguised the reality of the animals' existence. Stage- and mail-coach horses were treated badly and had a correspondingly short life, about three years on average, before they dropped dead in harness or were sent to the knacker's yard. The weight they were hauling, rather than the speed, was most wearing.

The more modern coaches weighed about 18 hundredweights empty, but when fully laden could be up to 2½ tons, and at Christmas, loaded with game and parcels, they were even heavier. In the summer of 1821 twenty

A mail coach changes horses at the Old White Lion, a substantial inn that may have once been a house or large farm. The ostlers uncouple the tired horses while fresh ones wait with their rugs on their hindquarters.

The coachman approves the choice of horses as the ostlers take out the leaders for his new team.

horses from William Chaplin's stable dropped dead in harness. When *The Peveril of the Peak* overturned near Bedford in 1836 it weighed 3 tons, and that was after some passengers and luggage had left it at Bedford.

Coachmen had to drive what horses were available. Most proprietors kept the best animals for the daylight stages for prestige reasons, but old and

A stagecoach descends a gentle hill without brake shoes or chains being used. The wheelers, the horses closest to the coach, were trained to lean back in their harness to slow the vehicle.

blind horses were harnessed up on night runs — 'black running' — when no one could see.

On well-managed runs the horses always ran the same stages, so they knew where they were going, and on more than one occasion a team safely completed a stage after the driver had fallen off drunk or suffered a heart attack.

The formula was one horse per mile for each route, so the number of horses needed was vast. The average price was £15–18 for horses in Ireland, £35–45 in London and £23–25 in the provinces, and to maintain one London to Edinburgh coach required over a hundred horses. William Chaplin owned 1,300 horses and at Hounslow, a major coaching centre that was the last change before and after London for the West Country stages, 2,500 horses were stabled by the various proprietors.

By the 1820s there was an improvement in the quality of horses and on some fashionable runs fine, well-cared-for animals were always used. These prestige teams were usually matched: for example the London to Blenheim coach always had four dapple greys, worth 200 guineas a team. By the 1830s public concern about animal cruelty was growing, and there were letters to the newspapers in protest about the treatment of the horses, but by then the age of the stagecoach was drawing to a close.

A coach passes the Woodman inn and its pleasure grounds on the Highgate road out of London.

# ON THE ROAD

SOME PASSENGERS enjoyed travelling by stage or found it an adventure, but on the whole it was thoroughly uncomfortable and whether or not it became a complete misery depended to a great extent on the weather, the other passengers and the individual traveller's temperament. Customer service and comfort were very low on the proprietors' agenda.

Travelling inside the coach gave shelter from the weather but passengers were squeezed into 16 inches or less of seat space each, with fellow travellers who might stink, be drunk, offensive or boring.

A song from an opera of 1761, called *The Stagecoach*, depicts the journey as a romp, but it would be anything but jolly for any 'nymph' who did not enjoy being 'squeezed and eased' by riotous young men.

In Coaches thus strolling,
Who wou'd not be rolling,
With Nymphs on each Side;
Still prattling and playing,
Our Knees interlaying,
We merrily ride …
Here Chance kindly mixes,
All Sorts and all Sexes,
More Female than Men;
We squeeze them, we ease them,
The Jolting does please them;
Drive jollily then …

Dickens stated flatly that 'Everyone dreaded stage coaches as a serious penance'. Jonathan Swift would have agreed. He wrote of a nightmare journey on the London to Chester stage where he was stuck between two fat elderly ladies, a 'bullying captain' and his lady, their small boy, who screamed and was sick, and Swift's own chubby landlord. Swift never travelled by stage again.

The frontispiece of *The Portfolio* ... the whole Calculated to Enliven The dull Hours of the Stage-Coach Traveller, Coffee-Room Lounger, Invalid etc. (1818). This volume is the early-nineteenth-century equivalent of taking a loaded e-book reader on a journey.

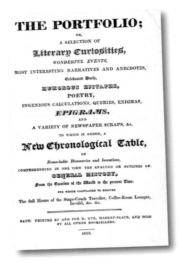

One of the surviving stagecoaches, the *Old Times*, is 41 inches wide inside, so that the six passengers, bundled up in outdoor clothing, had just under 14 inches of lateral space each. They perched on seats only 13½ inches deep with an 18-inch share of the knee room, and could only hope that their fellow passengers were both skinny and short.

The Honourable John Byng complained that being '... box'd up in a stinking coach, dependent on the hours and guidance of others, submitting to miserable associates and obliged to hear their nonsense, is great wretchedness!'

The interior of the *Old Times* stagecoach. The seats have been re-upholstered in authentic grey woollen cloth. It is possible to make out the top edges of both the glazed window (the 'glass') and the wooden shutter, both of which slide up and are fastened by a peg through a hole in a strap.

Count Kielmansegg described the initial awkwardness in his account of a visit to England in the 1760s:

> The first sight of people of different classes and sexes, who are perfectly unknown to each other, occasions, at the outset, deep silence, as nobody knows what to make of his neighbour or how to begin a conversation. At last someone begins to talk of the road and the weather ... A political discussion is sure to follow especially with English people.

In the early nineteenth century a German traveller, J. H. Campe, found his journey from Great Yarmouth to London a 'veritable torture'. They covered 124 miles in fifteen hours, with only one rest stop of half an hour.

Even the most urgent demands of nature had to be suppressed or postponed in order that there might not be a minute's delay in changing horses ... If a traveller wished to get down for a moment, he was faced with the danger that his luggage might be carried on to London without him. The coachman seemed to recognise no other duty than to arrive punctually.

While the horses are changed the inside passengers yawn and rub their eyes. One of the smartly dressed gentlemen on top is wearing the typical costume of the sporting Corinthians and may be hoping to take the reins himself.

The interior of the Holyhead to London mail coach, with the original upholstery. The padding is horsehair, long-lasting, but unyielding. The glazed window is raised and held by a strap and peg, and the flap beneath the window covers a large pocket.

Others enjoyed their journey. Washington Irving wrote in 1820 of a cheerful Christmas journey from Yorkshire. He enjoyed the company of the lively schoolboys on their way home for the holidays and marvelled at the loads of game birds and parcels.

Another American visitor, Joseph Ballard, was touring in 1815 and often found congenial travelling companions. Of one family party he wrote:

I was frequently regaled with the refreshments, which the gentleman had brought and was so polite as to offer me ... We travelled all night and at dusk I was not a little surprised at beholding my fair fellow traveller, who was quite a pretty girl, take off her bonnet, tie on her night cap, and leisurely compose herself to sleep in one corner of the coach, where she made quite an interesting appearance ... After going with almost incredible swiftness we arrived at Leeds at 6 o'clock in the morning, being at the rate of 8 miles and ½ each hour, including stoppages – a velocity with which I never desire to travel again.

The tollgate keeper has his nightcap on as the Mail passes through the gate in the moonlight.

The mail coaches were no more comfortable. The 1790s design was hung high on its springs and swayed alarmingly at speed. In 1798 the industrialist Matthew Boulton wrote: 'I had the most disagreeable journey I ever experienced ... The landlady at the London Inn at Exeter assured me that the passengers who arrived every night were in general so ill they were obliged to go supperless to bed ...'

The poet Samuel Taylor Coleridge arrived at Hatchett's Hotel, Piccadilly, in November 1817 after an all-night journey on the Bristol mail, 'coach-fevered, coach-crazed and coach stunn'd'. Later that year, after travelling on the same route, he wrote:

> ... the coach being quite full, all lusty men but one, and he together with one of the lusty travellers having great Coats on, or rather *huge* Coats that ought at least to have payed half-price, I was terribly cramped, my shoulders in a pillory and my legs in the stocks ... my feet and legs are more swoln than I ever remember them to have been on a similar occasion.

The male passengers have been turned off the coach to walk up a hill to spare the horses.

Outside seats gave passengers fresh air, better views and the opportunity to chat to the driver and guard. On the other hand it was more dangerous, was exposed to the elements, and on steep hills outside passengers might have to walk to spare the horses. The outside seats were over 6 feet from the ground, a dizzying perch if the vehicle was swaying.

Regulations permitted ten on the roof but reports show that this was often exceeded, as the American Benjamin Silliman discovered in 1805 when he travelled in a party of eighteen with six inside and twelve on the roof.

Kitchener advises: 'If circumstances compel you to ride on the outside of a Coach, put on Two Shirts and Two Pairs of Stockings, turn up the collar of your Great Coat and tie an handkerchief round it, and have plenty of dry Straw to set your Feet on.' He also recommends putting a parcel or clothes bag under the feet to keep them warm, or using a pewter water container that should be filled with hot water at stops. One ungrateful traveller complained of 'enough straw round my feet to conceal a covey of partridges'.

Miss Weeton, a nervous and impoverished governess, took her first holiday in 1824 at the age of forty-nine. She travelled outside for economy and was very cold on the journey from Liverpool to London. On the way back she indulged in some sightseeing: 'I was quite gratified with the sight of Oxford, although upon a coach and never descending.' She took a basket with cold tea, buns and biscuits, but as the evening progressed she became very cold and when they changed coaches a party of drunken Irishmen got on, one of whom stole her safe middle seat, so that she ended up crushed against the iron rail on the outside, very scared and reduced to tears.

There are nine passengers on top of this coach. The coachman is sitting on his folded benjamin for some extra padding.

QUITE FULL.

This print is entitled 'Quite Full', so it seems that those waiting may be out of luck. The outside passengers are wrapped up in blankets against the cold, with piles of straw around their feet.

Rain was always a misery. In 1822 Stanley Harris recalled sitting in front of a woman with an umbrella who kept knocking off his hat and would then 'shove it just below your hat so adroitly as to send a little stream of water down the back of your neck'.

Dry weather brought intolerable dust. Miss Weeton wrote:

The roads laid on McAdam's plan are better for carriages and easier for draft horses, but for human beings in dry weather, are almost beyond endurance; they are one continuous cloud of dust, blinding to the eyes, filling the nostrils, going down the mouth and throat by quantities to suffocation and completely ruinous to all decent clothing ...

Passengers also had the accompanying baggage to contend with. Their own required constant vigilance to protect it from damage, theft or, as the Wordsworths discovered in 1816, losses, 'owing to the carelessness of one of the Guards'.

Coaches carried packages for non-passengers as well, although generally parcels were less valuable than people, except at Christmas, when the carriage of parcels was very profitable and the Norfolk coaches arrived in London hung about with turkeys, geese, game birds and hares, with Christmas trees strapped on top.

Goods carried could be as varied as gundogs, haberdashery, bills of exchange and books, and the Kidderminster to London coach often carried heavy boxes of needles. When goods arrived in London they were handed over to porters, who were supposed to charge a fixed rate for delivery, but there were constant complaints about overcharging and delays.

There were, however, more unpleasant travelling companions than a plucked turkey or a barking gundog. Body-snatchers found the stagecoach a convenient method of delivering their wares to surgeons, sometimes disguised as boxes of books. *The Times* reported on 28 January 1837 that a human skeleton was found at the Birmingham coach office, where it had remained for two years, being undeliverable because it bore 'no known address'. A surgeon stated that the body of a man 'had been doubled up in the box in the manner in which it was usual to pack subjects for dissection'.

The seats at the rear of the *Old Times* stagecoach, showing the rails that were all a passenger had to hold on to. The seat backs are hinged and could be folded down, as here, to make loading and unloading the baggage in the middle easier.

The Norwich to London mail carries its traditional load of game birds and evergreen trees for Christmas.

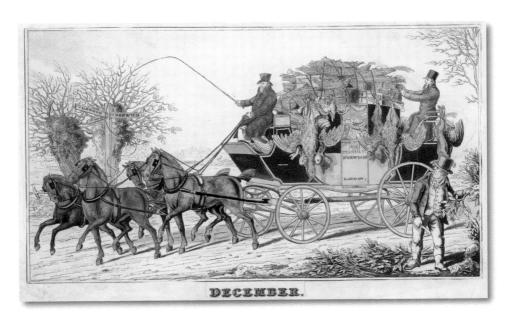

DECEMBER.

# INNS

A T FIRST STAGECOACHES ran during the day and stopped at night, a routine known as 'inning', although travellers were not guaranteed a bed and might have to make do with a chair while innkeepers reserved the best beds for private carriage owners.

By the nineteenth century the pressure for speed meant coaches kept going day and night, reducing the profits for the inns. In the latter days of the London to Edinburgh run there would be only three meal stops in two days. Macaulay thought that the faster the coaches went, the worse the inns became, for landlords lost the business from people sleeping over or enjoying a leisurely meal, and had to extort the maximum profit by charging exorbitant prices and serving poor food to passengers who had no time to complain or look for alternatives.

Many writers criticised stagecoach dinners. Surtees described:

> ... a little, dark, dingy room ... the table, which was covered by a thrice-used cloth, was set out with lumps of bread, knives and two or three pronged forks laid alternately ... Presently the two dishes of pork, a couple of ducks, and a lump of half-raw, sadly mangled cold roast beef, with waxy potatoes and overgrown cabbages were scattered along the table.

Food was often slow in arriving and very hot, but passengers were forcibly prevented from taking any with them when the coach departed, leaving the uneaten food to be served up to the next arrivals. As a result, eating could become an unmannerly scrum and one definition of a true gentleman was that he would 'behave courteously at a stagecoach dinner'.

Passengers frequently stayed at the terminus inns overnight in order to catch the early morning departures, or northbound travellers might start from the Peacock or the Angel in the village of Islington, the first stop out from London. At these establishments the quality of food, at least, was better.

Ralph Rylance, in *The Epicure's Almanac*, reports that 'A most excellent dinner, or any other repast' was to be had at the Gloucester Coffee House in Piccadilly, the terminus for the western mails, and that nearby at Hatchett's Hotel 'capital dinners and suppers are served to a numerous and respectable set of customers'

Some inns provided local specialities – Oliver's Hotel in Bodmin served Cornish cream and potato pasties, bubbling hot and handily wrapped up in white paper to carry away.

The beds were another matter, however, and experienced travellers, such as Mrs Elton's sister in Jane Austen's *Emma*, packed their own bed linen, as 'An excellent precaution'.

Benjamin Silliman, while staying at the Belle Sauvage, was 'bit so terribly with buggs again this night, that I got up at 4 o'clock this morning and took a long walk by myself about the City till breakfast time'. John Byng complained that when he stayed at the Crown at Ringwood in Hampshire in 1782, 'Of all the beds I ever lay in, that of last night was the very worst, for there could not be more than fifty feathers in the bolster, and pillow, or double that number in the feather-bed.'

Not everyone was dissatisfied. Generally foreign visitors found more to admire than British passengers. In 1827 Count Pecchio enjoyed the fires, the feather beds, the hot water and the free newspapers. 'English inns would be real enchanted palaces, if the bill of mine host did not appear to dispel the illusion', he concluded.

Washington Irving spoke of his pleasure when he 'entered and admired for the hundredth time, that picture of convenience, neatness and broad

An eighteenth-century inn yard with a stagecoach due to depart. A woman in the booking office rings a bell and the landlord presents a bill to a guest.

A stagecoach breakfast. The passengers are eating a hasty meal while two of the gentlemen are changing neck cloths and boots, and another is receiving a shave. The coachman, having reached the end of his run, has come in to solicit his tips.

The coach comes into the inn yard with an ostler already at the horses' heads as the guard swings down to unload baggage.

honest enjoyment, the kitchen of an English inn'. He praised the fires, the welcome, the attentions of the landlady and her maids, and the food, while Prince Pückler-Muskau in 1826 approved of the washing facilities and the neatly dressed servants, although he disliked the level of tipping.

More inns were needed as the coaching network grew. They were seldom purpose-built and were often converted farmhouses or decayed manor houses, with convenient stabling and outhouses.

Some coaching inns were of considerable size. This is the George in Buckden, Cambridgeshire, on the Great North Road.

Many reverted to their old function when the railways killed off their trade.

The business could be hectic. In the village of Liphook, Hampshire, twenty-six coaches stopped to change horses every twenty-four hours. The innkeeper of the Anchor inn bought from the local baker, pie shop and butcher and employed over a hundred local people in the inn and on the three farms that supplied the stables and kitchen. Entire village economies depended on the coaching trade.

# DANGERS AND ACCIDENTS

As well as the discomforts and inconveniences of the coach, and the expense and variable quality of the inns, travellers were well aware of the dangers of stage travel. Fears that brain damage would result from the terrifying speeds of over 5 mph proved unfounded, but criminals, severe weather, drunk drivers, racing, overloading and steep hills were real perils.

The *London Gazette* in 1684 carried an advertisement offering a reward after the Northampton stage was 'set upon by four Theeves, plain in habit but well-horsed', and in one week in 1720 every stagecoach into London from Surrey was robbed by highwaymen. But the days of the feared highwaymen were coming to an end in the early nineteenth century as the coaches became faster, the guards were better armed and mounted patrols were put on the roads. However, they persisted longer in Ireland, where the roads were of a poorer standard and the slower coaches made easier pickings. In 1808 a coach lined with copper and advertised as bullet-proof was tried on the Dublin to Cork road.

Porters might be thieves themselves or be conned into handing parcels over, while 'Peter-hunting' was the specialised crime of lifting parcels and trunks from stagecoach boots, usually in foggy weather or at night. Pickpockets rode on the stage or frequented the inn yards.

Mail coaches offered the richest pickings because they often carried currency, and in 1827 the Birmingham mail was robbed of £20,000. Robberies from stagecoaches reached serious proportions and in 1825 *The Times* reported that 'perhaps £100,000, transmitted by coaches, are known to have been stolen within the last few years'. The proprietors were responsible for losses in law, but getting them to pay up usually required litigation.

Theft was alarming but rarely put passengers' lives at risk. The weather was more lethal, especially for those outside. Jane Austen's nephews Edward and George arrived in Southampton in October 1808, '... very cold, having by choice travelled on the outside, and with no great coat but what Mr Wise,

Opposite:
The stagecoach and horses are completely trapped in a drift and the passengers flounder through the snow.

53

the coachman, good-naturedly spared them of his, as they sat by his side. They were so much chilled when they arrived, that I was afraid they must have taken cold.'

The boys were fortunate, for passengers frequently died of exposure or were too rigid with cold to climb down on arrival. In March 1812 the Bath coach to Chippenham arrived with two outside passengers frozen to death and a third dying.

Snow was a particular hazard in Scotland and Wales, with drifts over the heads of the outside passengers in 1827 and 1836. It was less of a risk in England, although the Christmas of 1836 was very bad, with the network in chaos, coaches abandoned and nothing in the right place. On 8 December *The Times* reported a shortage of horses in London because no coaches could get in. Drivers, guards and horses were exhausted. Near Bristol one hundred passengers were stranded in two small inns, and St Albans was gridlocked with coaches.

Fog caused numerous accidents after coaches had left towns, where they were guided by running linkboys with torches, and flooding was a frequent danger in spring and autumn. Usually the coachmen drove through the water, but that left the interior awash and the passengers soaked. High winds could blow down trees or overturn coaches. One coachman, Moses Nobbs, would open both doors and tie them back so that the wind went right through, which must have been uncomfortable for the inside passengers.

Dangerous as the weather might be, human factors were the cause of most accidents, top-heavy coaches being the most frequent cause of overturning. The earlier straight-perch (chassis) coaches were more likely to tip over because of their high centre of gravity, and it was not until the bent perch came in during the 1830s that the passenger compartment was lower slung and the vehicle more stable.

In 1770 *The Annual Register* recorded:

> Thirty-four persons were in or around the Hertford coach this day, which broke down by one of the braces giving way. One of the outside passengers was killed on the spot, a woman had both her legs broke ... and very few of the number either within or without but were severely bruised.

Sir St Vincent Cotton, driving too fast, overturned the Cambridge *Star*, broke the leg of Calloway, England's premier jockey, and paid £2,000 in compensation. The Reverend Atterbury of Christ Church, Oxford, whose hobby was to ride on the box, 'to see the working of a well-appointed coach and to sit behind a fine team skilfully handled', died when the coach overturned and his skull was crushed, and in 1833 there was a dreadful accident to the *Quicksilver*, which overturned as it was leaving Brighton.

Stagecoach passengers watch in alarm as a driver loses control of his gig.

Cartoonists enjoyed depicting the victims of accidents flying through the air or revealing their underwear, but a coach accident was a serious matter and people were frequently killed or injured.

Passengers were flung out into the gardens along the Steine and on to the spiked railings.

Drunkenness was a frequent cause of reckless driving, and night driving was the most dangerous of all. On 19 December 1835 Edward Jenkins, drunk, drove the London mail over a 121-foot drop near Llandovery and into a river. Miraculously, everyone on board survived, unlike the unfortunate Methodist preachers travelling on the *Royal Fleece* from Huddersfield to Sheffield for their annual conference in 1823. The driver galloped his team down Shelley Bank with the wheels unlocked and the coach overturned on a bend. Two were killed.

One combination of overloading and poor visibility led to a stagecoach proprietor having to pay £200 in compensation when a naval captain sued him for damages after suffering concussion and a broken arm. The original coach was changed for a smaller one, with all the luggage piled on top so that it became unstable. They were then about to set out in the dark when the passengers pointed out that there were no lamps, and the captain announced that he was not putting his life at risk as he had a wife and children. The proprietor declared, 'What do I care for your wife and children?' and then fell into a furious argument with the coachman, who refused to move off until lamps were fetched. According to the *Star* of 21 December 1815:

> The coachman, apparently in an ill humour, then mounted the box and drove off with the greatest rapidity. Mr Hulme turned round, and said to the guard, 'If he drives at this rate, he will overturn us.' The vehicle had not proceeded many yards before this prophecy was fulfilled …

Braking on hills was especially perilous. Sir Henry Parnell in his *A Treatise on Roads* cautions:

> Few travellers by stage coach are aware of the risk they run of losing their lives in descending hills. A coachman must be thoroughly well skilled in his business, naturally cautious, and at all times sober. The wheel horses must be not only well trained to holding back, but very strong. If a pole breaks … when a heavily-laden coach is descending a steep hill, at a rate exceeding six miles an hour, an overturn is almost inevitable, by reason of the coach overpowering the horses. Hence it is that ninety-nine out of every hundred coach accidents which happen are on hills.

One of the pair of lamps on the *Gay Gordon*. These provided the only illumination at night, other than the moon and starlight. Other than showing the position of the coach to other road users, they would have been of little help to the driver, who had to rely on his horses and his own knowledge of the road.

Going down a steep hill on a frosty morning with the wheelers down on their haunches to brake the coach.

Racing between rival coachmen, or by amateur whips, led to many spectacular crashes. Mrs Mountain ran the *Tally Ho!* fast day coach to Birmingham but William Horne put his *Independent Tally Ho!* on the same route. The rival coachmen would race the whole way until, on May Day 1823, the *Independent Tally-Ho!* beat all records, driving the 109 miles in seven and a half hours, an average speed of 14½ mph, which left the passengers terrified.

At least that coach arrived safely. In 1820 the Chester mail raced the Holyhead mail down the hill out of St Albans. Galloping flat out, the horses swerved into each other and the Holyhead coach hit the bank and overturned. One passenger broke his neck and two others were severely injured. Both coachmen were found guilty of wilful murder, although the sentence was only one year's imprisonment.

Horses were easily startled. Dr John Knyveton recorded in his diary what happened when the off-leader shied at a hen flying across the road:

> ... the coach lurches, and then tumbles into a ditch, the road being soft with mud at that point. The ditch was deep so none was hurt bad; but two women inside began to scream most piercing, being badly shook in their wits; and one gentleman was thrown clean off the road into the hedge.

The stagecoach with the grey horses appears to be the challenger in this race on the Brighton road as the guard blows his bugle and the inside passengers stare out in alarm.

On 15 November 1836 the Bristol mail was standing outside the Gloucester Coffeehouse in Piccadilly without the coachman. When the coach in front started, the Bristol horses bolted after it towards Hyde Park Corner. The porter loading luggage on the roof was thrown off, and the runaway caused chaos all along Piccadilly. The horses were finally stopped by the drivers at a cab rank, who discovered that the two ladies inside had fainted. The coach was too damaged to continue but a substitute was found and was on its way with only twenty-five minutes' delay.

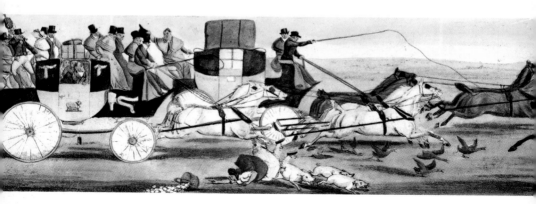

The horses jib as they cross Newmarket Heath during a thunderstorm at night.

The most dramatic occasion when the horses were panicked was in October 1816 when a lioness escaped from a travelling menagerie and attacked the Exeter *Quicksilver*, outside an inn near Salisbury. No one was injured, although the horses were clawed. The mail was delayed by only forty-five minutes.

A stagecoach and a hunt arrive at a tollgate at the same time.

# THE END OF THE ROAD

THE HEYDAY of the stagecoaches in Britain was 1825–45. Improvements in the vehicles and the roads enabled the entire country to be served by fast, regular coaches just at the moment when the fatal threat to the industry appeared. In 1825 the Stockton & Darlington Railway opened, and in 1830 the new Liverpool & Manchester Railway was an immediate success, carrying over thirty thousand passengers a month.

At first there was no recognition of the threat, except to the carriage of goods and the mail. Railways were regarded as dangerous and smelly, and only one of the great coach proprietors, William Chaplin, foresaw the future. He bought railway shares and used his vehicles to carry passengers and goods to the stations. His rival, Sherman at the Bull and Mouth, refused

Coachmen, put out of work by the railways, complain that they are starving.

Ladies & Gents! I am werry sorry to turn out in this here shabby manner, but you see I've been knocked off my perch - druve off the Road! to no mistake -vith all these here Boys about me. to not vun on'em as can you're a livelyhood - Ladies & Gents! My Drag & the Boys Shayses, & I may say, the whole consarn has been regularly Smashed by them Railway chaps! so pray remember the Coachman !

To THE RAILWAY

to see the threat until he had lost over £7,000, at which point he too bought railway shares.

Passengers soon overcame their fears and saw that railways were superior for speed, price and carrying capacity. Passengers could travel from London to Edinburgh at a penny a mile, a total fare of £2 as opposed to £7 by coach, and twice as fast.

For a while it seemed that stagecoaches could convert to steam, and in 1831 the first regular steam-driven carriage service, from Cheltenham to Gloucester, drove over 3,000 miles using steam carriages designed by Goldsworthy Gurney. Walter Hancock ran a steam omnibus between Paddington and the City and another service in Brighton, but these pioneering attempts were ended when the turnpike trusts, in league with the stagecoach proprietors, raised the tolls for steam carriages to the prohibitive level of £2, in contrast to horse-drawn coaches at 2s, unwittingly signing the death warrant of their own businesses.

In 1838 an Act of Parliament permitted mail to be carried on trains. The last stagecoach from London to Birmingham ran in 1839, from London to Bristol in 1843, and London to Plymouth in 1847. By the late 1840s it was all over for the long-stage routes, with a devastating effect on the thousands employed in the subsidiary industries. Bustling little coaching towns became silent villages, and the road network went into a sharp decline that only the rise of the motorcar in the twentieth century reversed.

The short-stage routes continued longer in remote areas and in the suburbs, carrying passengers to and from the railway stations. Stagecoaches survived in Scotland and Ireland until the 1870s. The specialist coachbuilders kept some business by building private drags for sportsmen and driving clubs, and in 1851 the census showed that there were still 16,839 coachmen, guards and postilions not in private service.

But the stagecoaches were effectively dead and they were rapidly transformed in the public imagination into objects of romantic nostalgia with a glamour that would have astounded the cold, uncomfortable, grumbling passengers of the previous two hundred years.

This steam carriage, constructed by Goldsworthy Gurney in the late 1820s, was driven by the 'guide' or 'engineer'. It was powered by coke and could reach 8–10 mph, carrying six inside and twelve outside passengers.

The ignominious end of the road for a stagecoach.

# FURTHER READING

Adkins, Roy & Lesley. *Eavesdropping on Jane Austen's England*. Little, Brown, 2013.

Benford, Mervyn. *Milestones*. Shire Publications, 2002.

Burgess, Anthony. *Coaching Days of England*. Elek, 1966.

Cunninton, Phillis and Lucas, Catherine. *Occupational Costume in England*. A & C Black, 1976.

Dickens, Charles. *Sketches by Boz* (various editions).

Harper, Charles G. Numerous titles including: *Stagecoach and Mail in Days of Yore; The Great North Road: The Bath Road; The Dover Road.* (c. 1900) Various e-book and print-on-demand versions available.

Mountfield, David. *Stage and Mail Coaches*. Shire Publications, 2003.

Rylance, Ralph (edited by Janet Ing Freeman). *The Epicure's Almanac: Eating and Drinking in Regency London 1815*. British Library, 2012.

Selway, Neville C. *The Regency Road: the coaching prints of James Pollard*. Faber, 1957.

Simond, Louis (edited by C. Hibbert). *An American in Regency England: the journal of a tour in 1810–1811*. Maxwell, 1968.

Sparkes, Ivan. *Stagecoaches and Carriages*. Spurbooks, 1975.

Tristram, W. Outram. *Coaching Days and Coaching Ways*. E. P. Publishing (1973 facsimile of 1893 edition) E-book versions available.

Wilkinson, Frederick. *Royal Mail Coaches*. NPI Media Group, 2007.

Woodward, C. Douglas. *The Vanished Coaching Inns of the City of London*. Historical Publications Ltd, 2009.

Wright, Geoffrey N. *Turnpike Roads*. Shire Publications, 2008.

# PLACES TO VISIT

## COLLECTIONS CONTAINING ORIGINAL STAGE OR MAIL COACHES

*Red House Stables Carriage Museum*, Old Road, Darley Dale, Matlock, Derbyshire, DE4 2ER. Telephone: 01629 733 583.
Stage and mail coaches and accessories; various horse-drawn vehicles, including those used in Jane Austen film and TV adaptations; driving lessons and carriage rides

*The Mossman Collection*, Stockwood Discovery Centre, London Road, Luton, LU1 4LX. Telephone: 01582 548 600.
Website: www.lutonculture.com/stockwood-discovery-centre/gardens-and-galleries/mossman
Large collection of horse-drawn vehicles including a mail coach.

*Swingletrees Carriage Driving Centre*, Swingletree, Wingfield, Nr. Diss,
    Norfolk, IP21 5QZ. Telephone: 01379 384 496.
    Website: www.swingletree.co.uk
    Carriage collection including the London to Norwich Royal Mail.
*Birmingham Museums: Museum Collection Centre*, 25 Dollman Street,
    Birmingham B7 4RQ. Telephone: 0121 303 0190.
    Website: www.bmag.org.uk/Museum-collections-centre
    Visits by appointment (see website). Contains the *Old Times* stagecoach.

## POSTAL HISTORY AND MAIL COACHES

*The British Postal Museum and Archive* (Archive: Freeling House, Phoenix Place,
    London WC1X 0DL; Museum store: Unit 7 Imprimo Park, Lenthall
    Road, Loughton, IG10 3UF) Website: www.postalheritage.org.uk
    At present there is no permanent museum collection on general view
    but the archive contains many items of interest relating to the mail
    coach era and the Museum Store which contains a reconstructed
    mail coach can also be visited by appointment. Various venues and
    collections detailed on the Collections & Catalogue tab. Enquire
    before visiting.

## COACHING INNS

*The Bell Inn, Stilton*, Great North Road, Stilton, Peterborough, PE7 3RA.
    Telephone: 01733 241066.
    Website: www.thebellstilton.co.uk/bell-inn-history
    An historic coaching inn on the Great North Road with a fine inn sign
    and linked to the development of the famous Stilton cheese.
*The George Inn (Southwark),* The George Inn Yard, 77 Borough High Street,
    Southwark, SE1 1NH. Telephone: 020 7407 2056.
    Website: www.nationaltrust.org.uk/george-inn
    The only galleried coaching inn left in London. It is still a working
    public house.

## CARRIAGE MUSEUMS

*Arlington Court: National Trust Carriage Museum*, Arlington, near Barnstaple,
    EX31 4LP. Telephone: 01271 850296.
    Website: www.nationaltrust.org.uk/arlington-court
    A large collection of nineteenth-century horse-drawn carriages in the
    grounds of a fine National Trust Regency house.
*Tyrwhitt Drake Museum of Carriages*, Mill Street, Maidstone, Kent.
    ME15 6YE. Telephone: 01622 602847.
    Website: www.museum.maidstone.gov.uk/tyrwhittdrake
    Interesting collection of horse-drawn carriages. No stage or mail coaches.

# INDEX